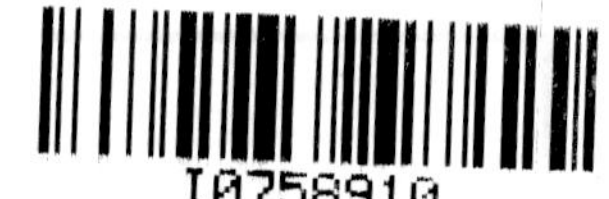
I0758910

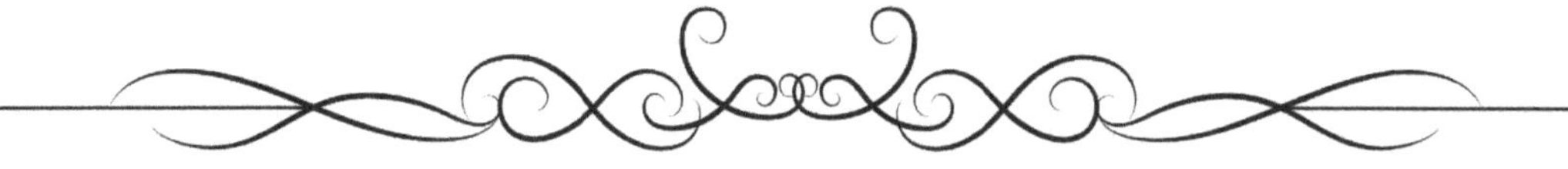

This Coloring Book Belongs to ....

....

....

....

....

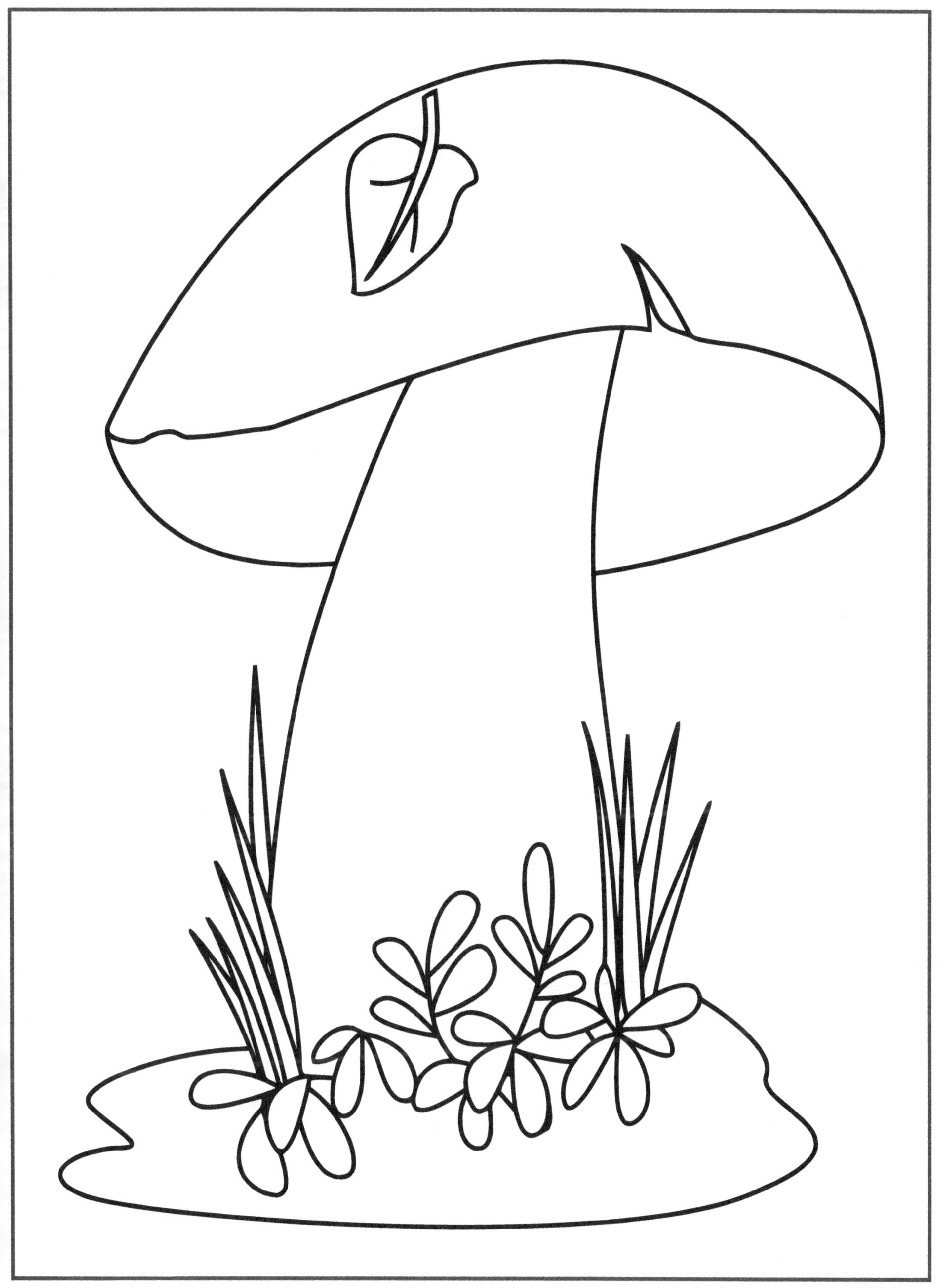

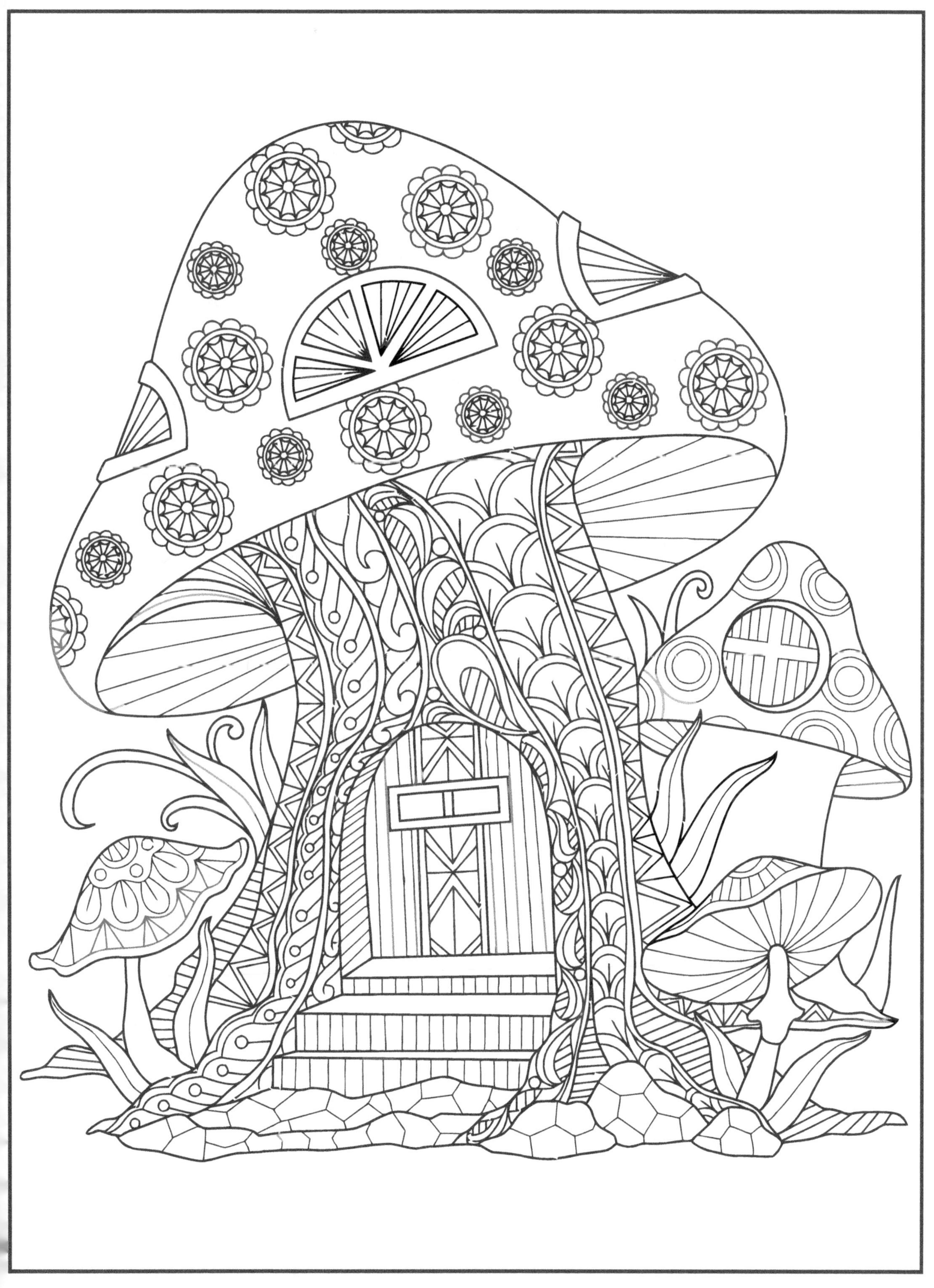

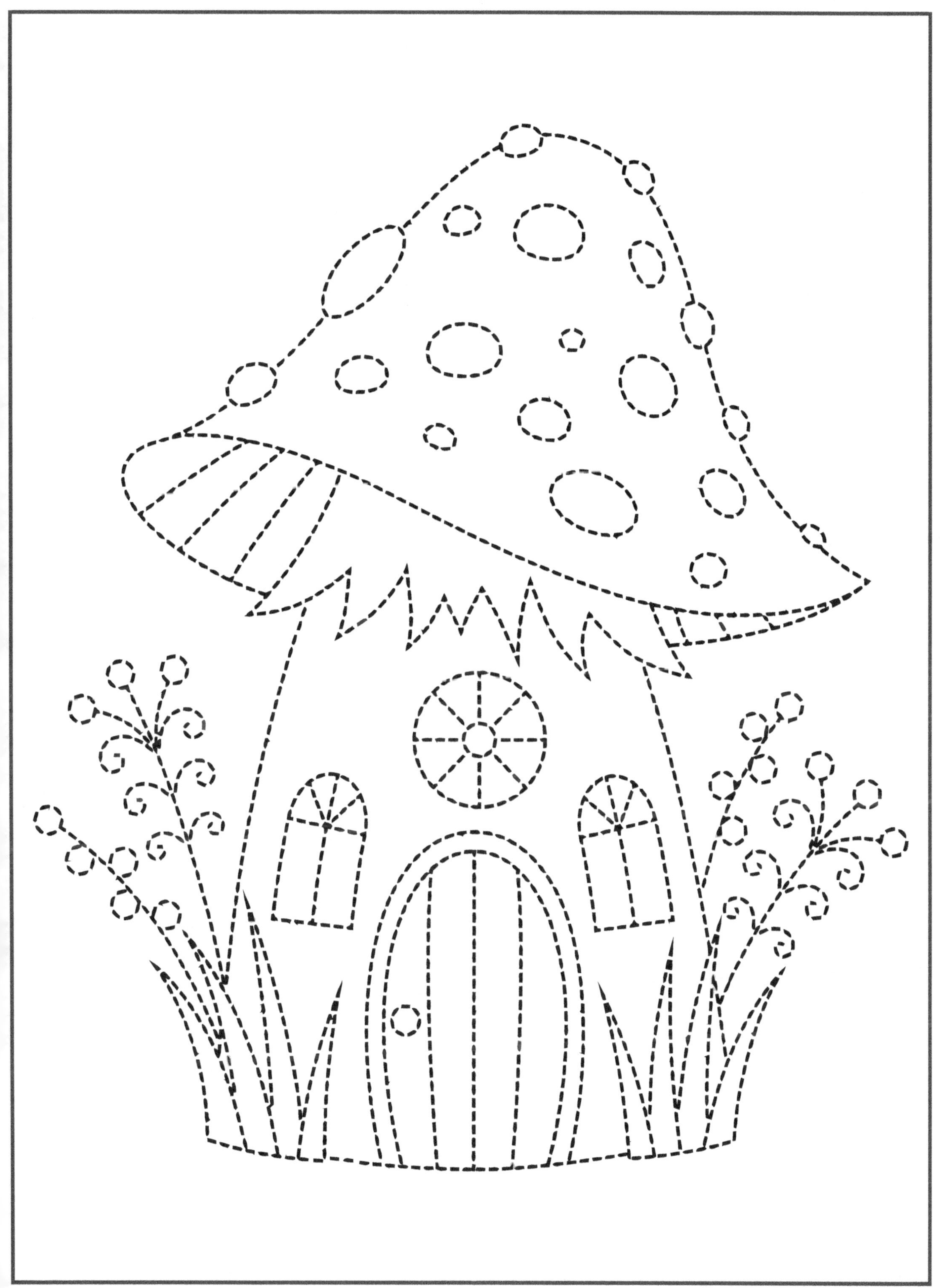

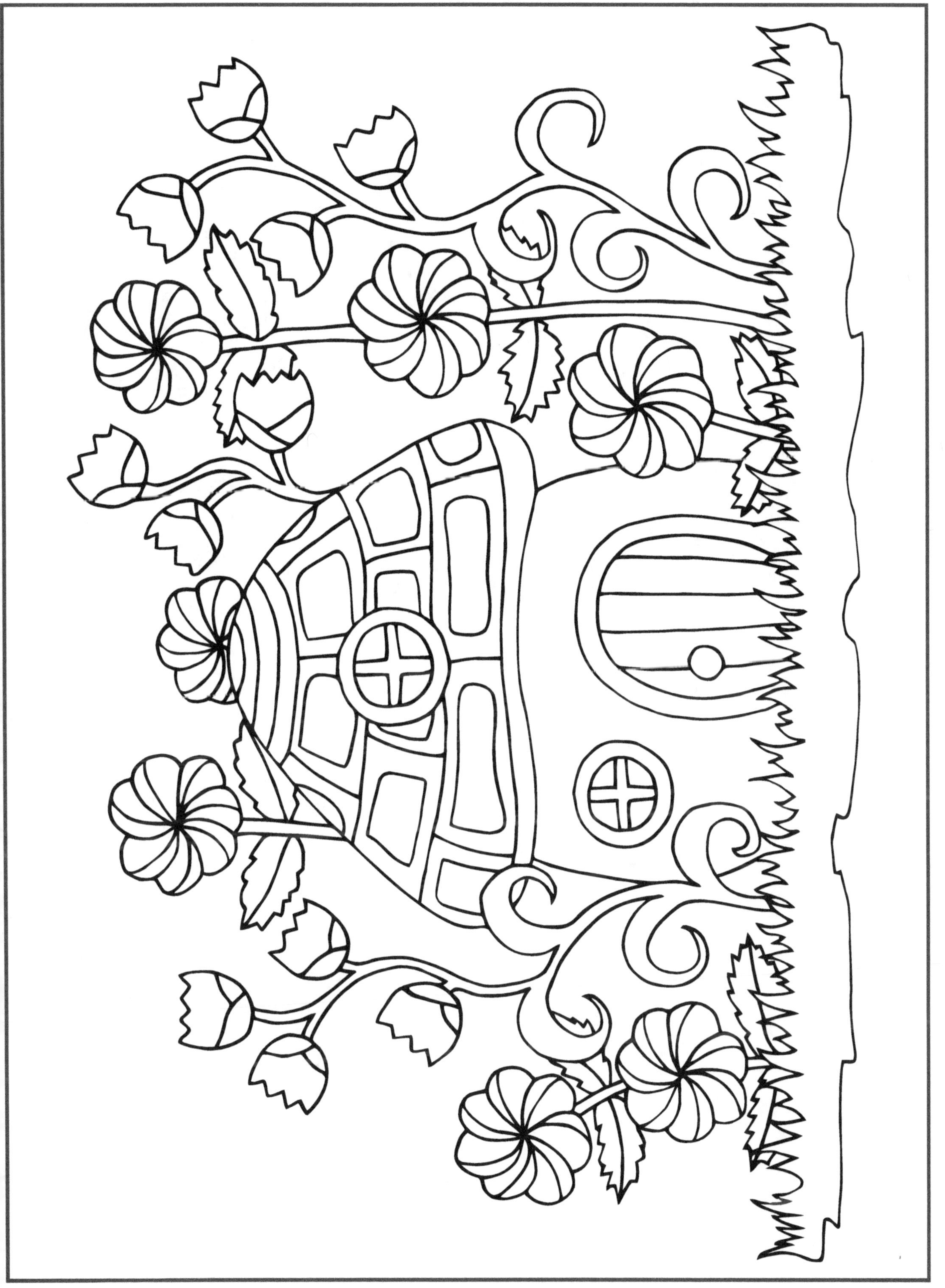

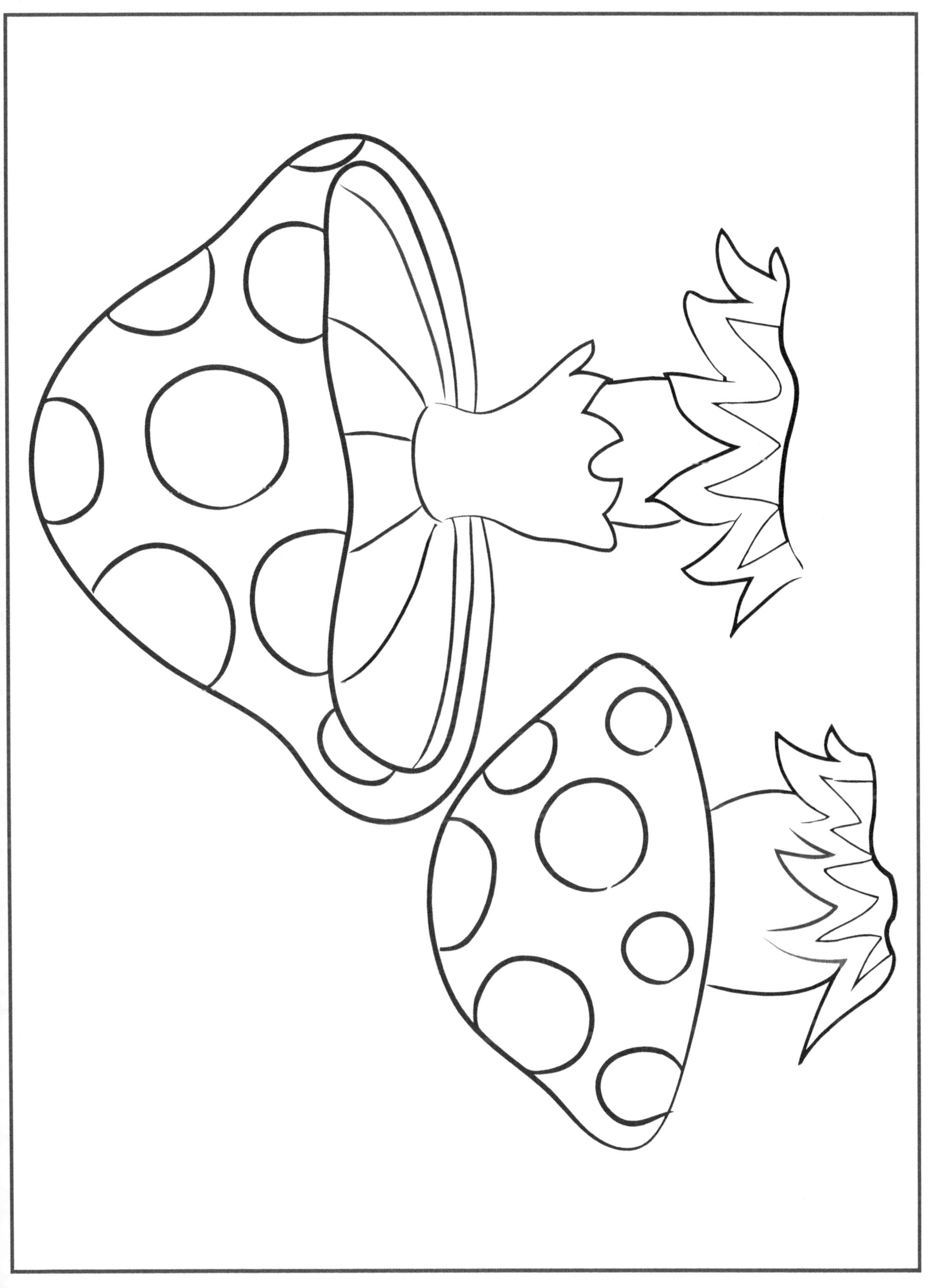

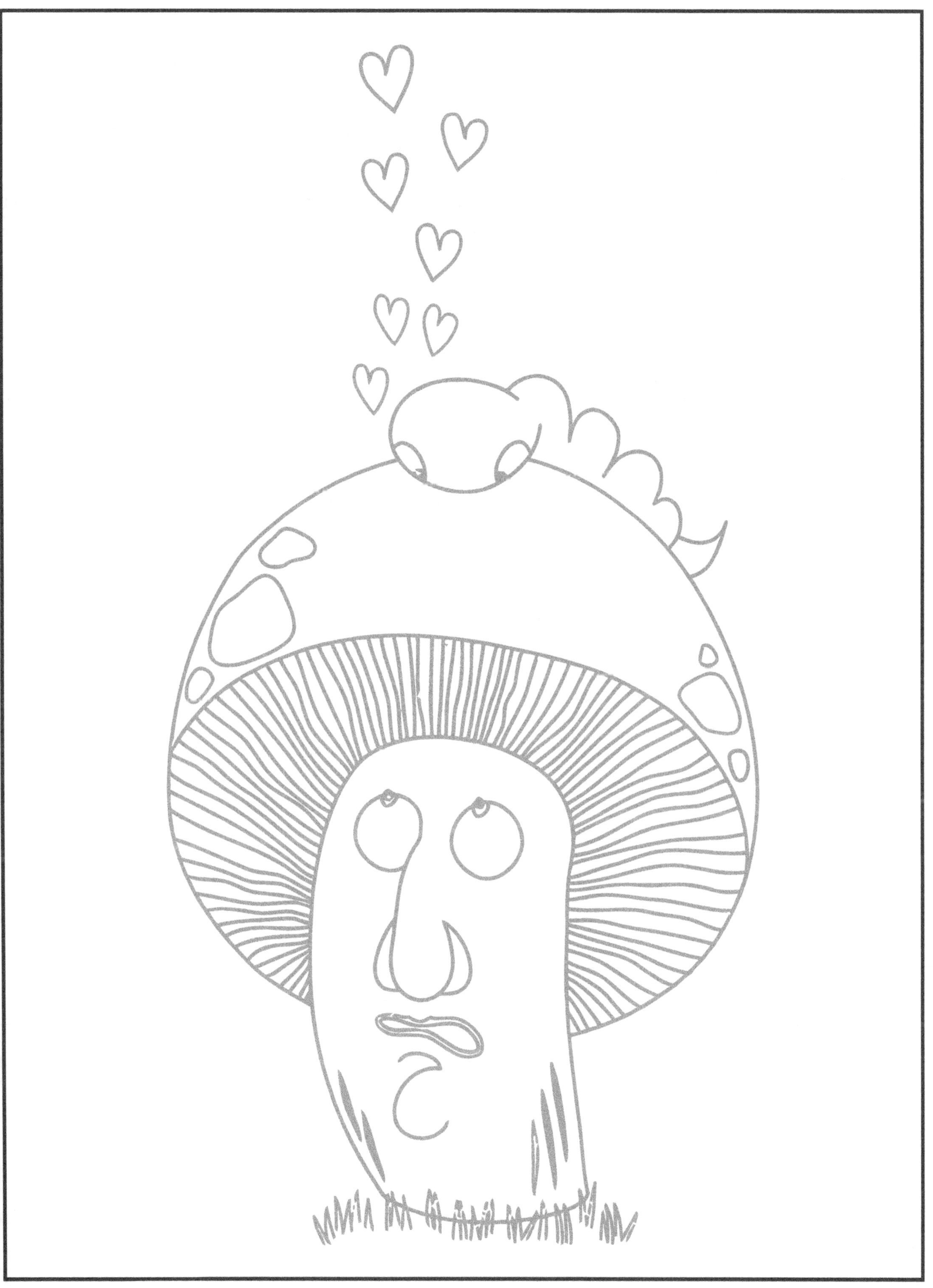

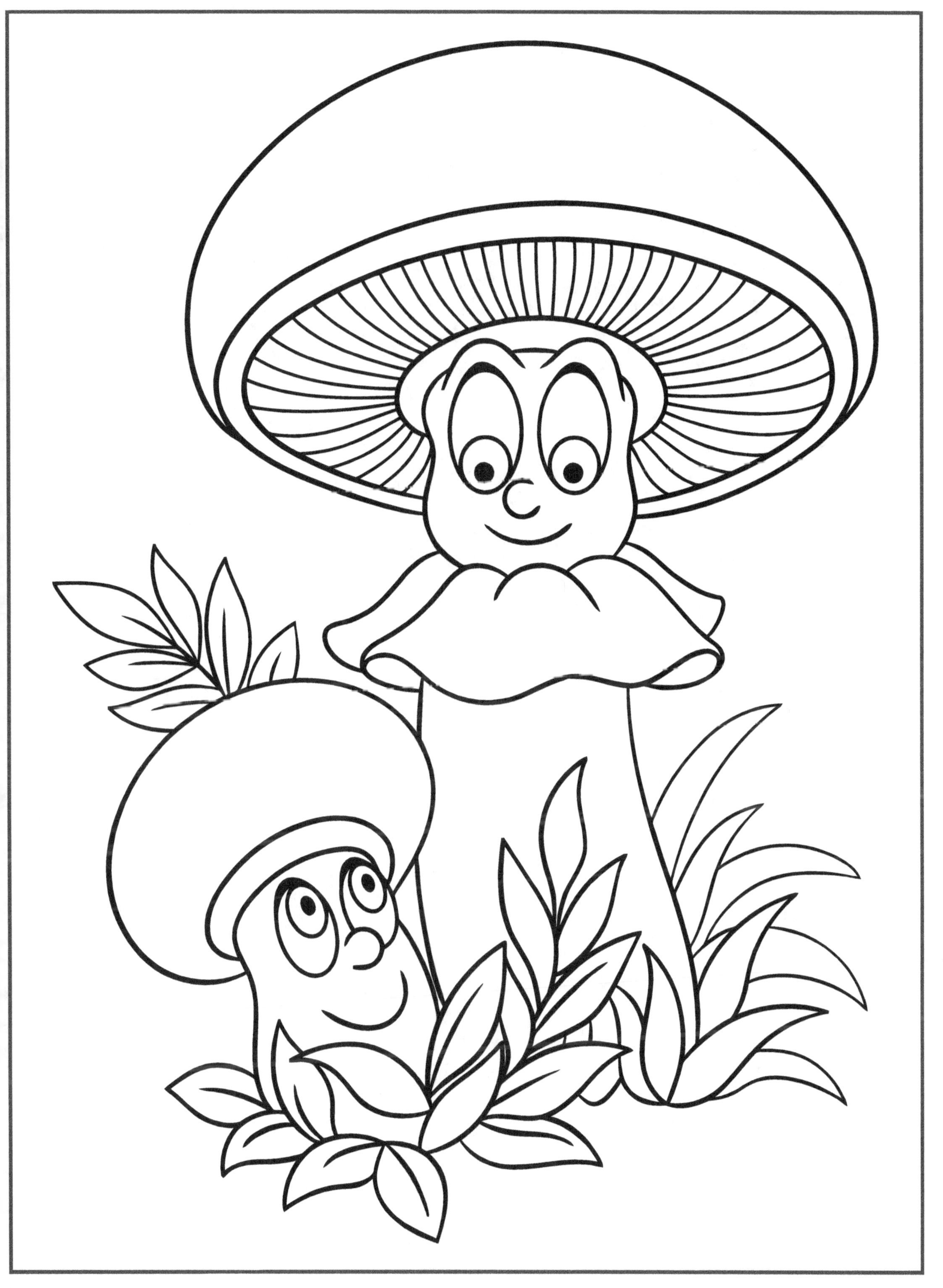

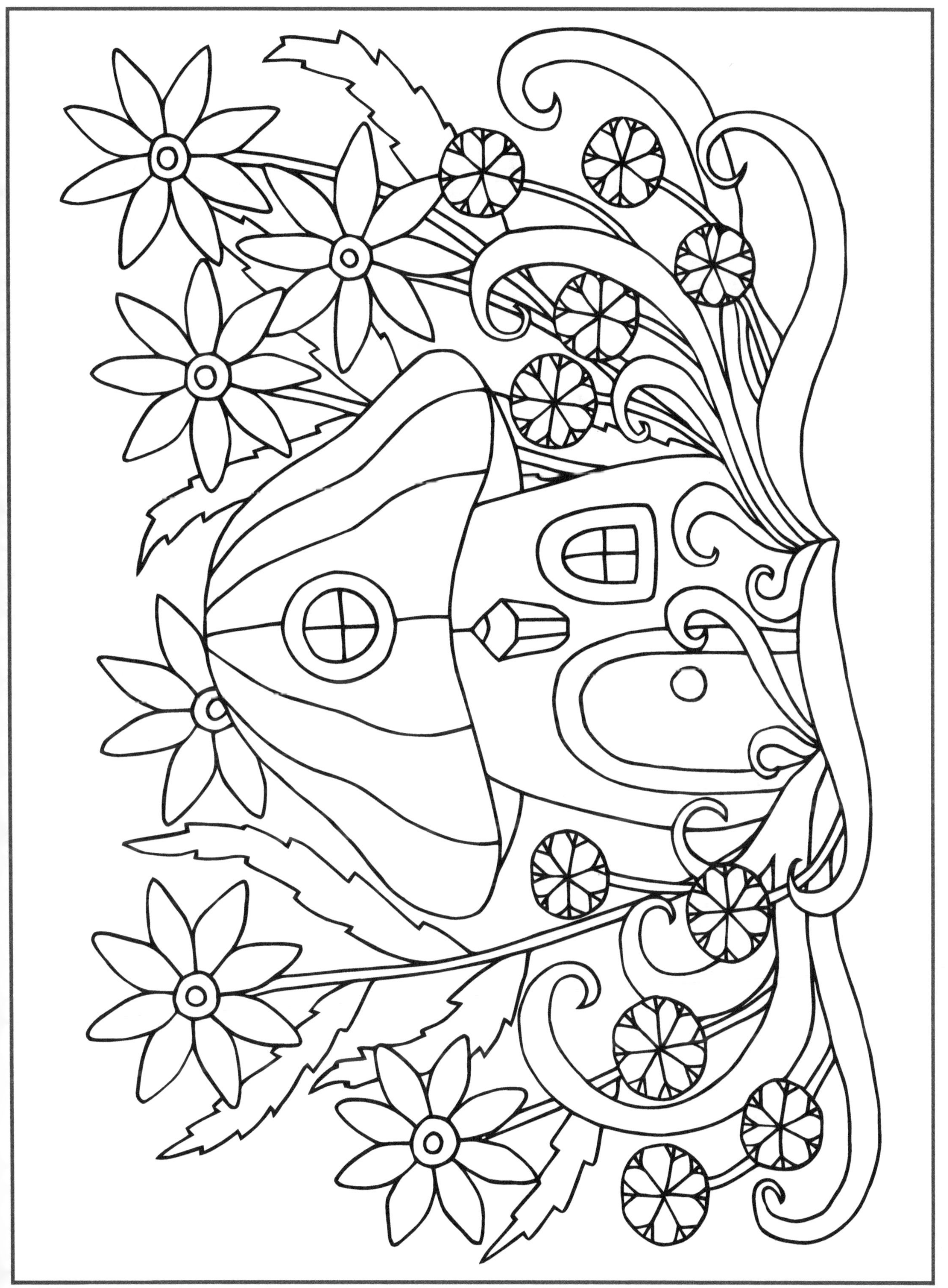

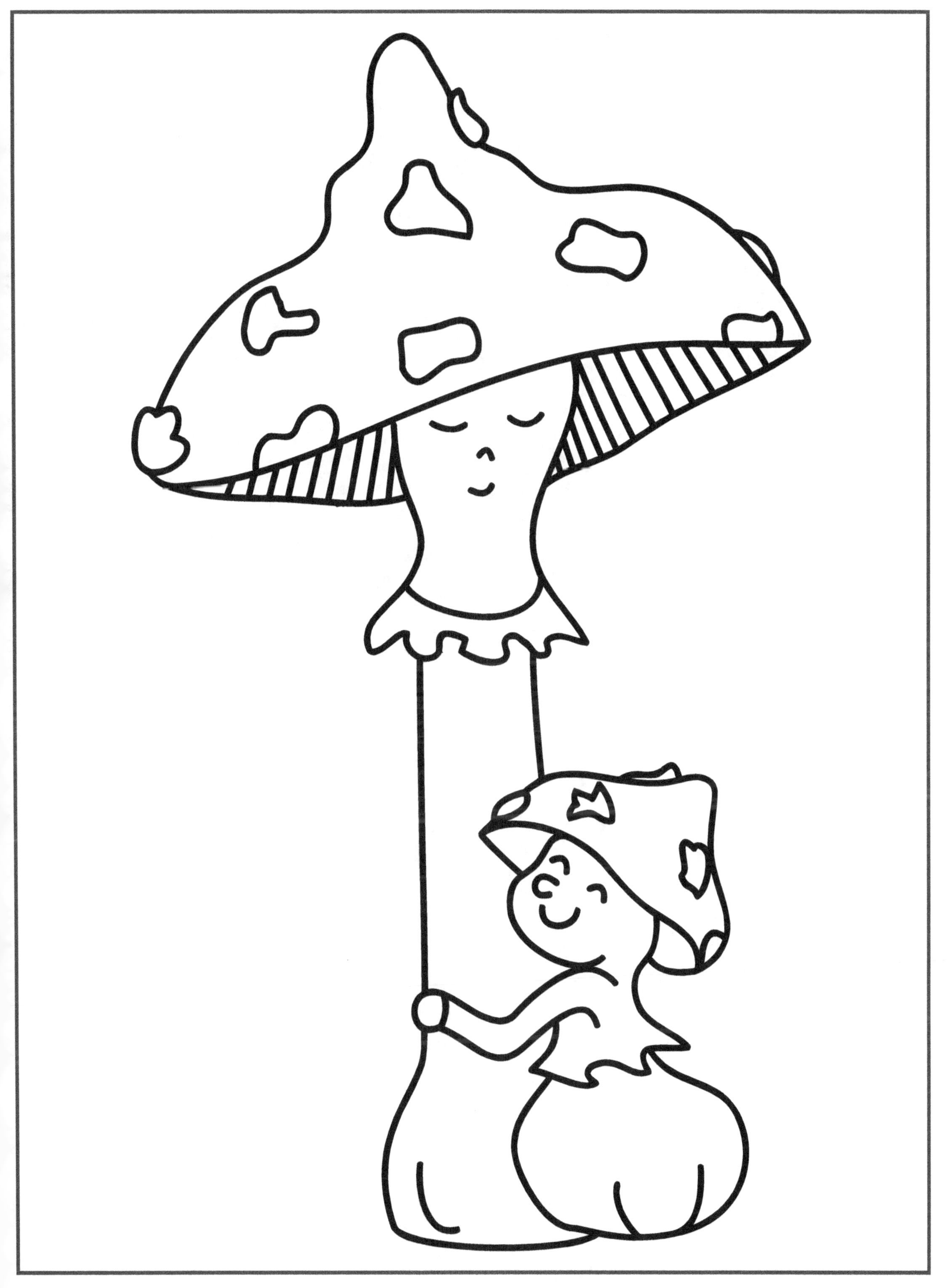

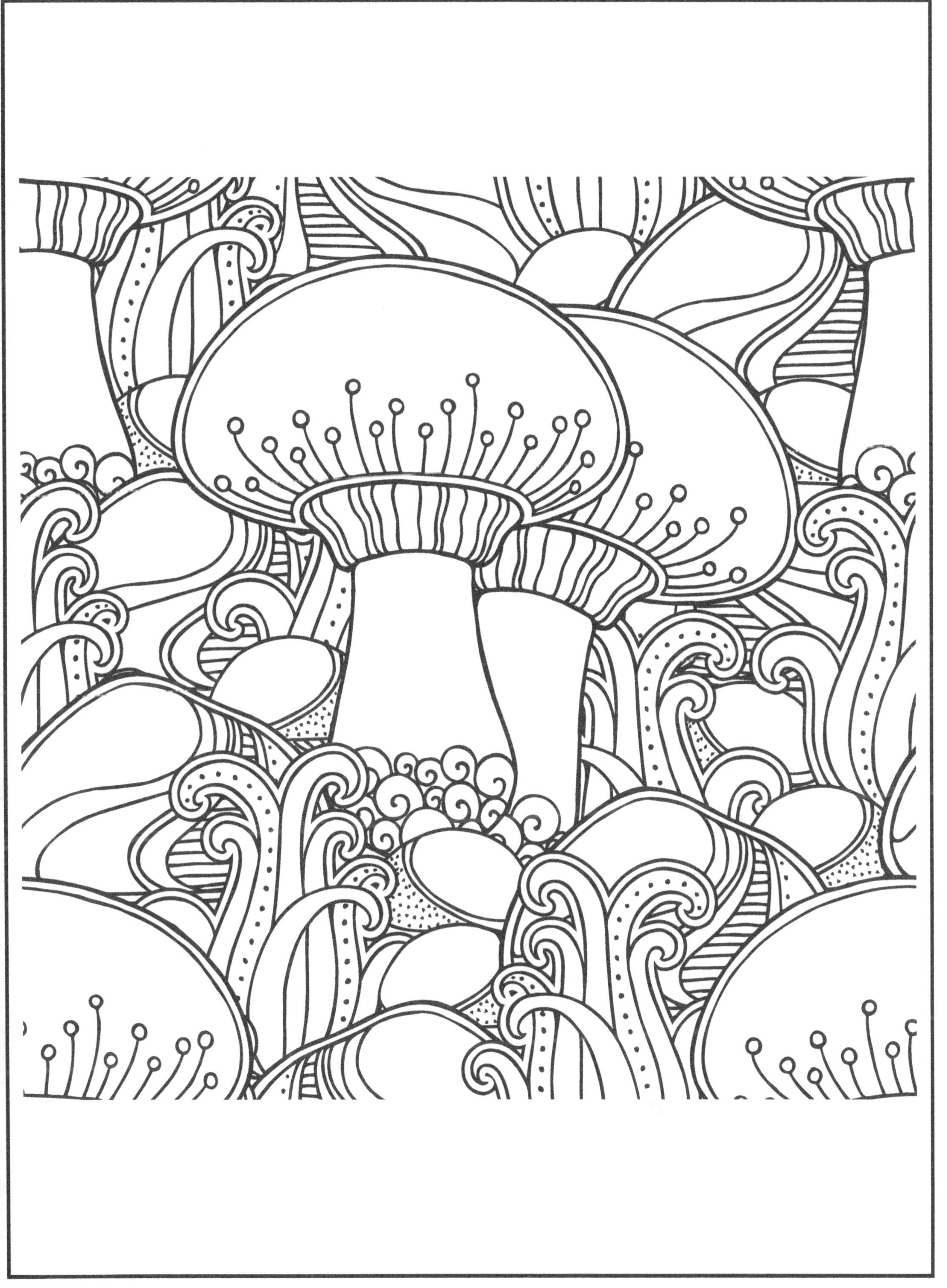

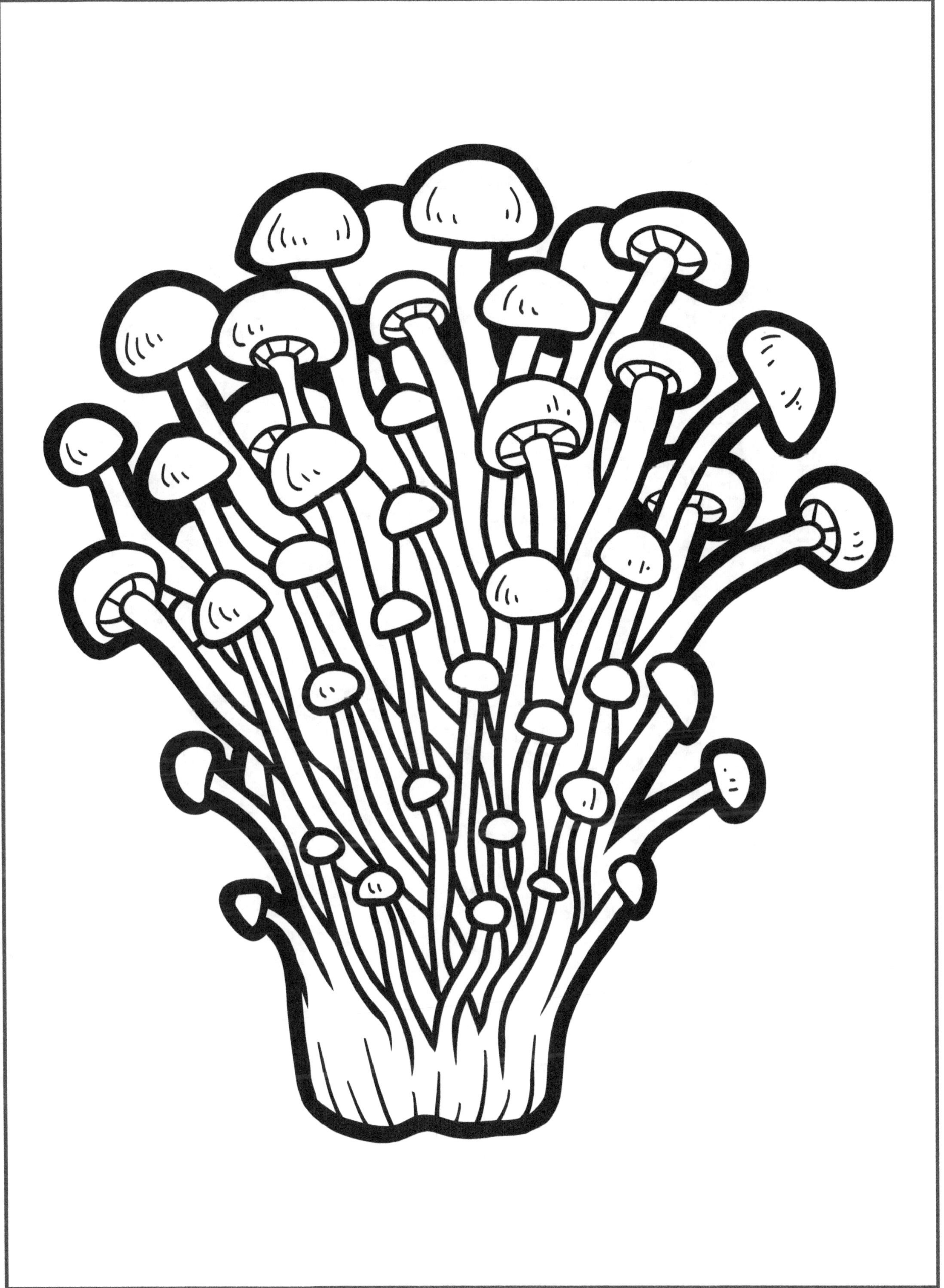

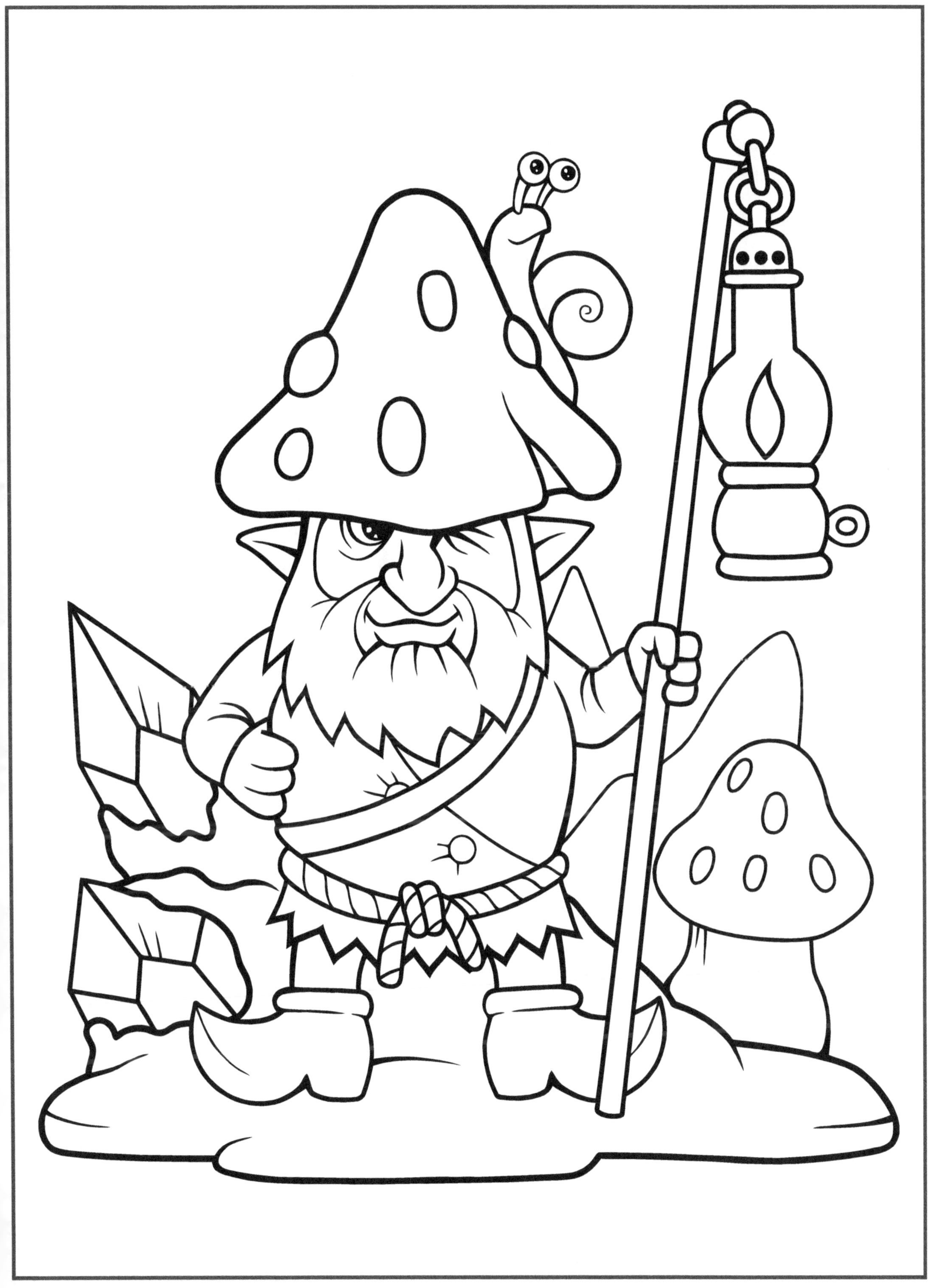

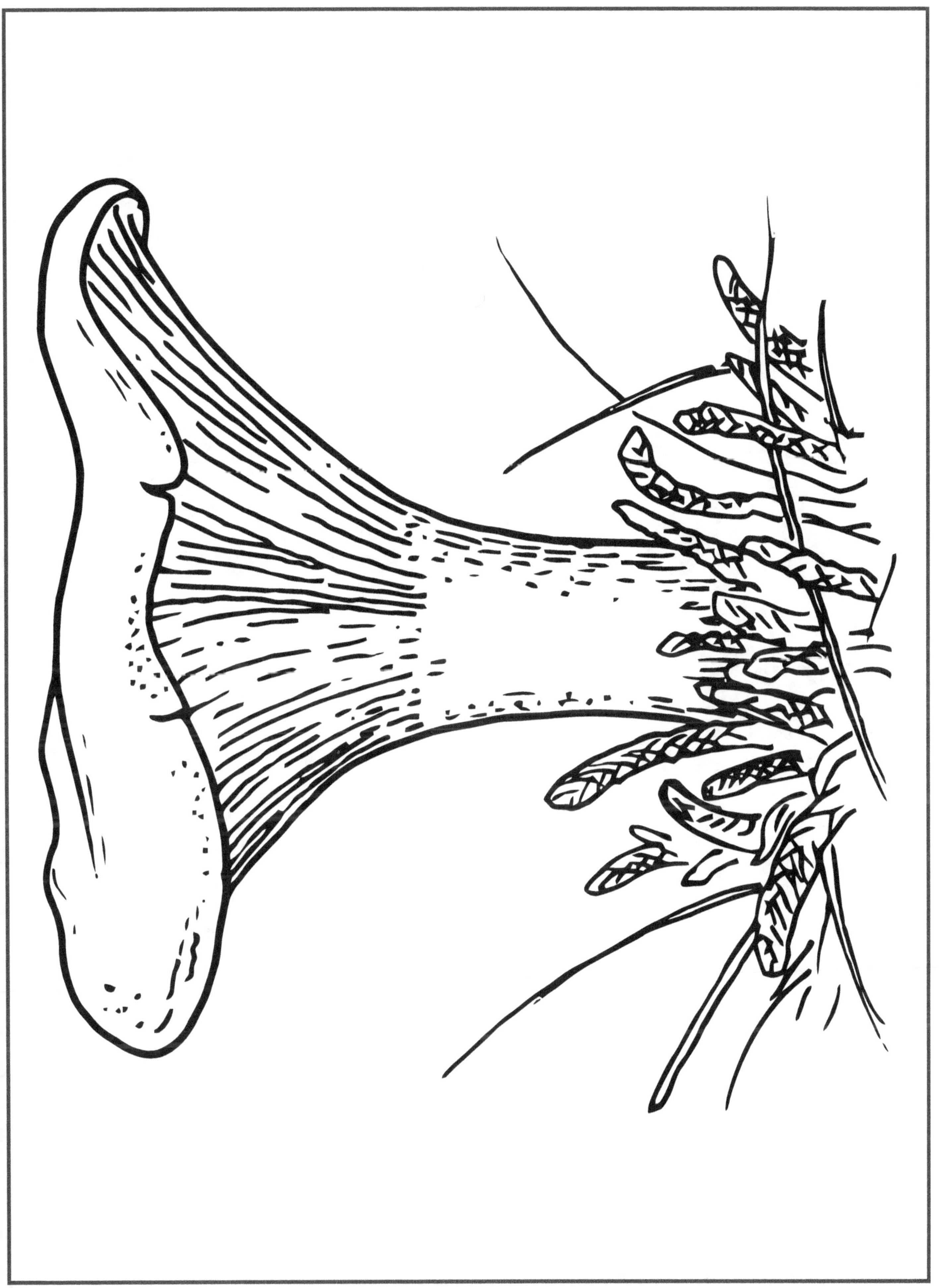

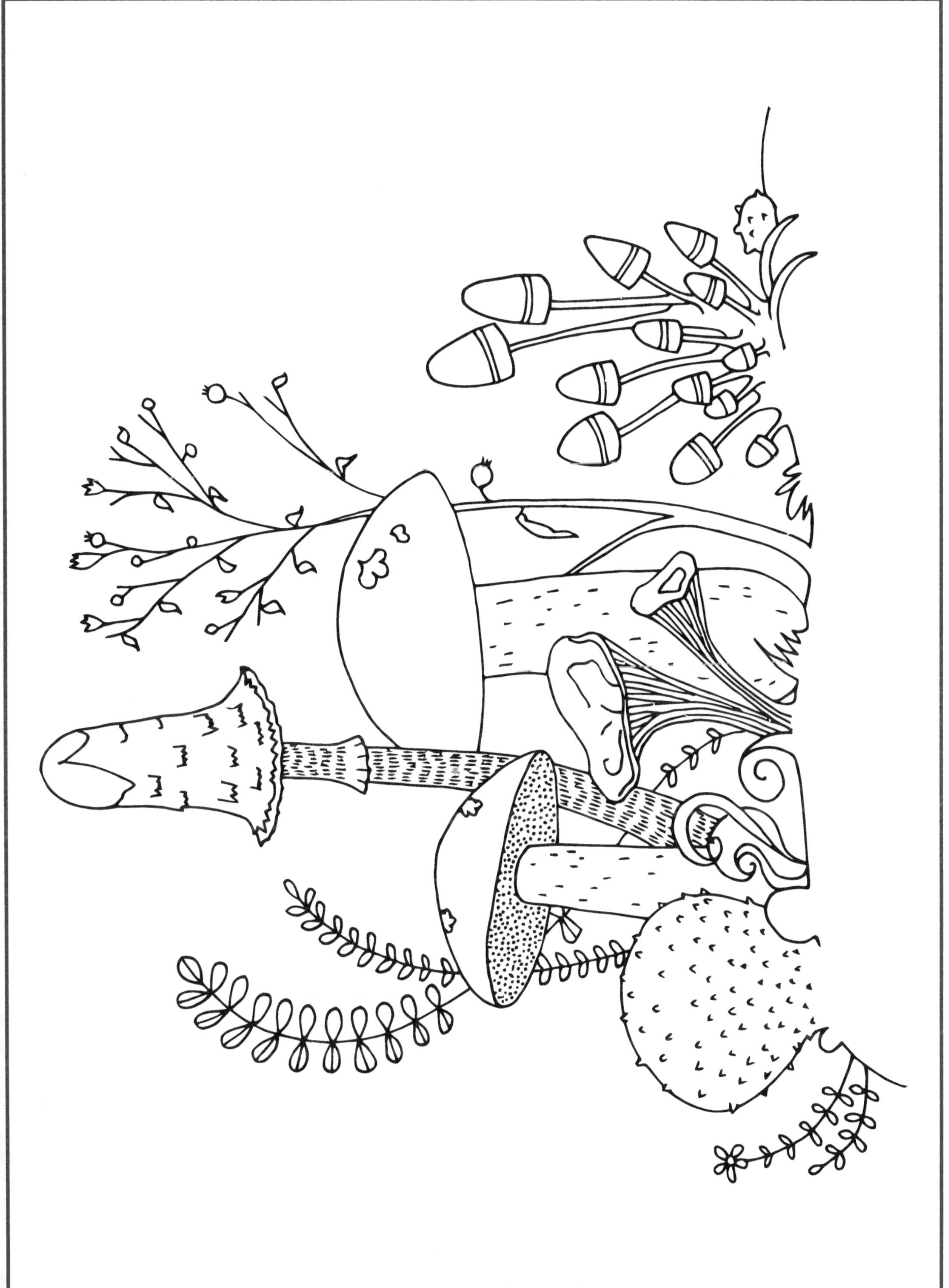

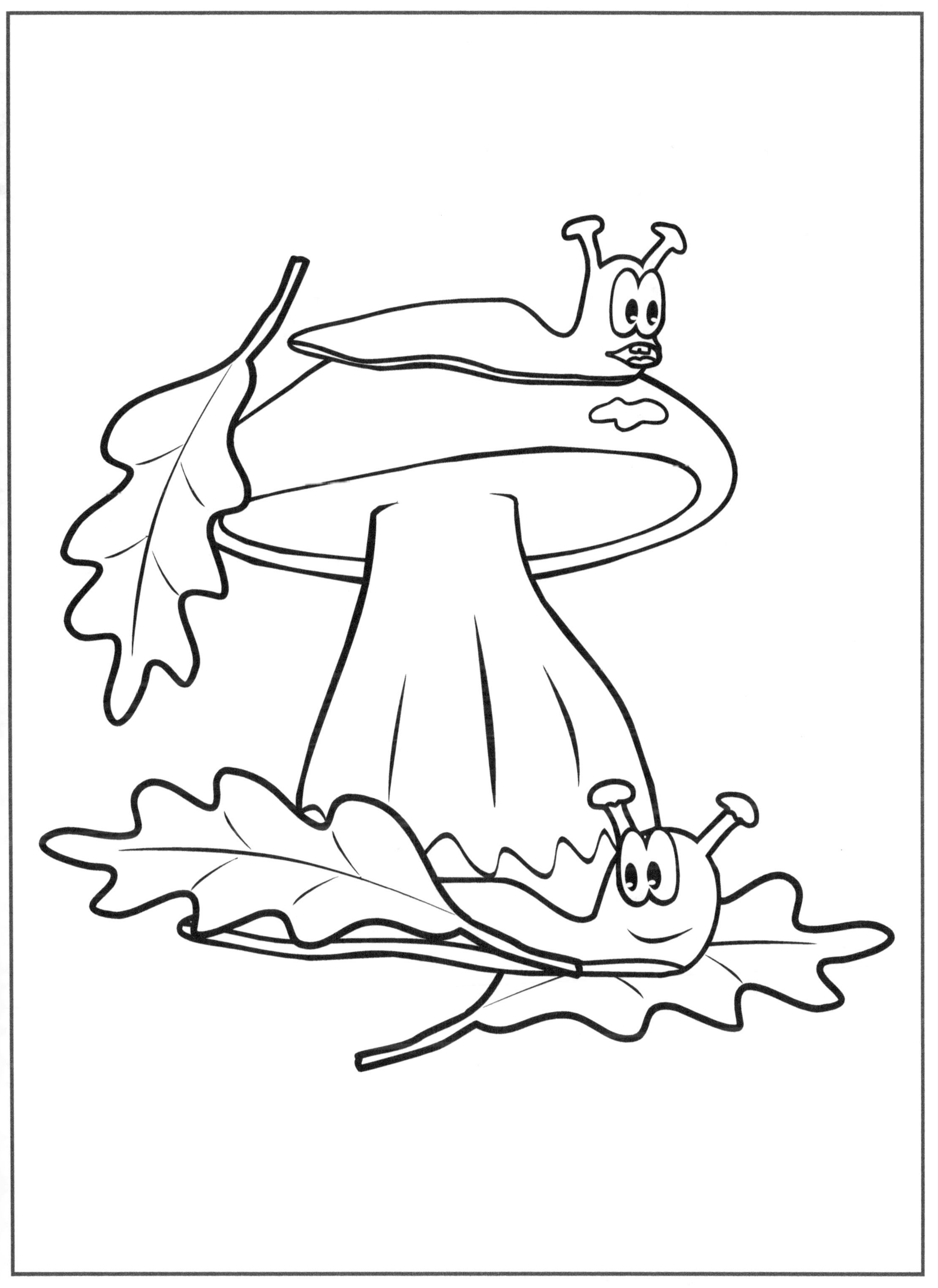

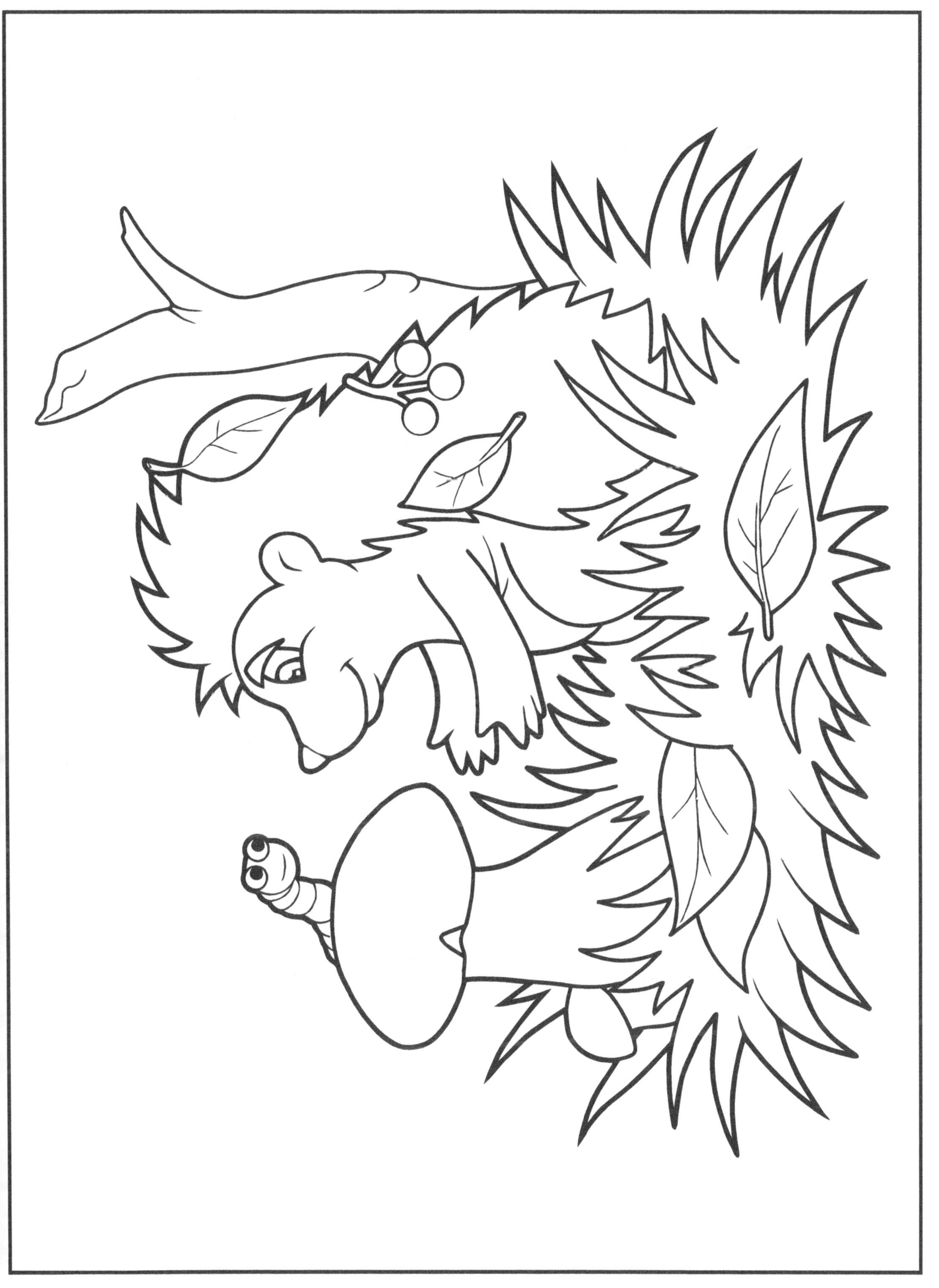

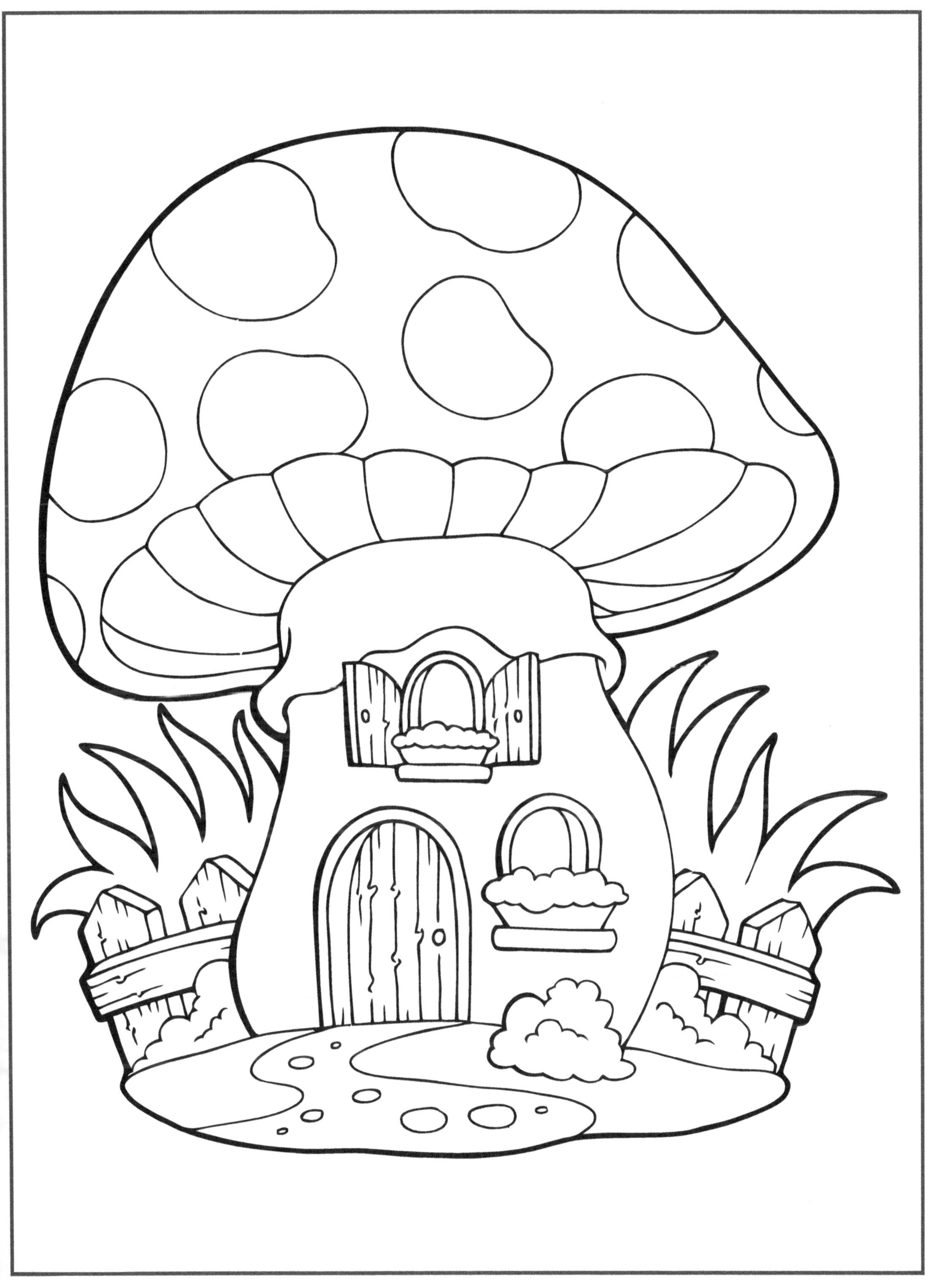

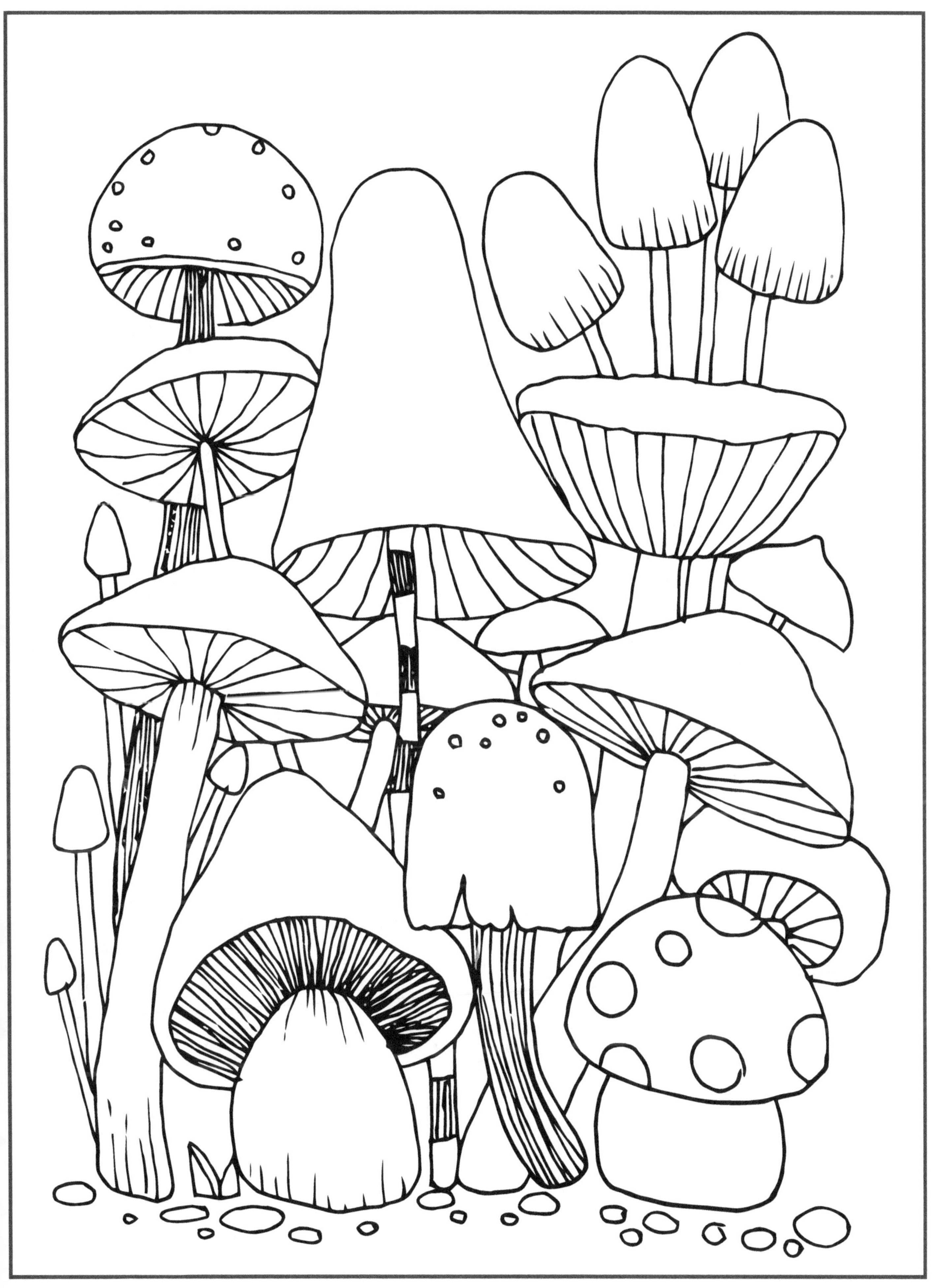

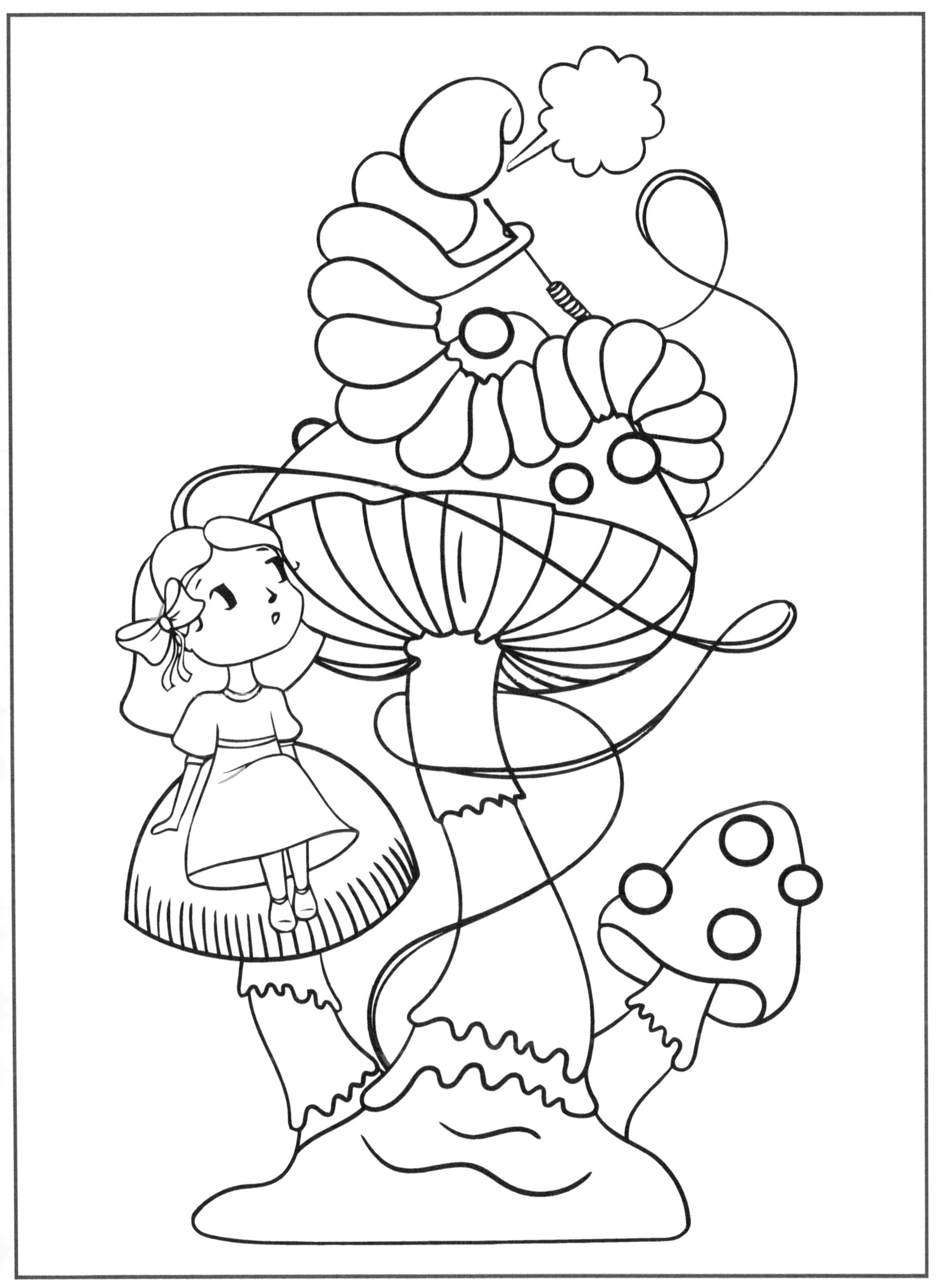

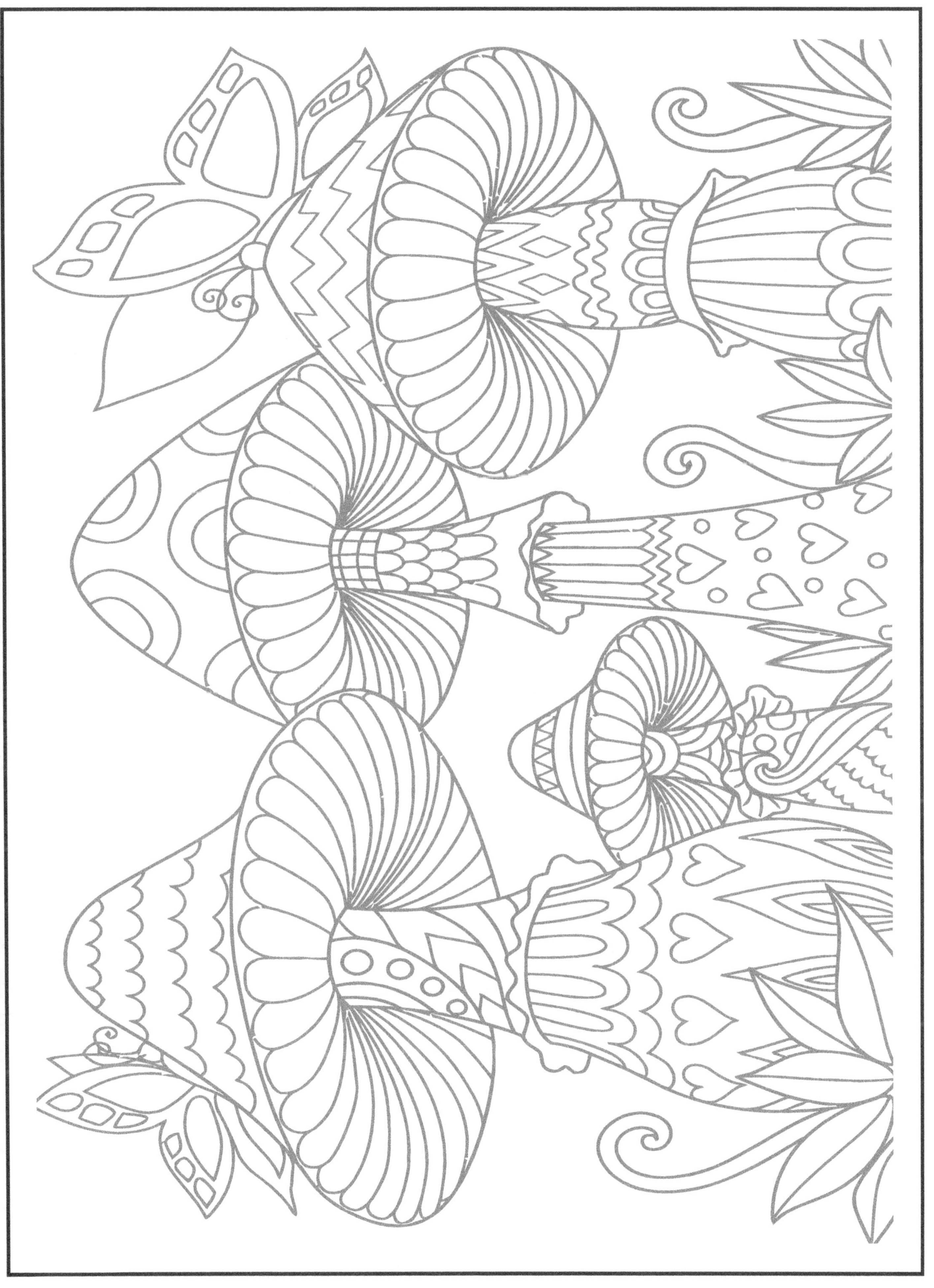

www.ingramcontent.com/pod-product-compliance
Lightning Source LLC
Chambersburg PA
CBHW082333270726
48658CB00018B/3263

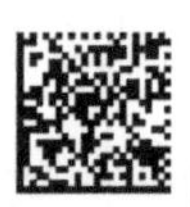